FOREWORD

A great revolution is under way in the world of finance and the way the countries could transact with each other.

A revolution that could be the greatest in the history of banking and finance. ...There is a lot of wealth, more than most people can imagine. The recent approval of ETF's on 10th January 2024, by the SEC in the US has opened the doors for investments to come in Crypto currencies in 2024 especially Bitcoin, and as of End of January 2024, about 5 Billion$ of investments were seen in the ETF's in last 20 days of January alone, this is the just the beginning or tip of the ICEBERG!!, The investments could be in Trillions in just 1-2 years.

Why Crypto currencies: The use of crypto for conducting business presents a host of opportunities and challenges. As with any new frontier, there are both strong incentives and unknown dangers. That's why individuals or Corporations intent on investing should have two things: a clear understanding of **why** they should invest and secondly **the process** they should follow.

The Investment funds like Blackrock, Fidelity, Ark Investments and many others listed below strongly feel there is a raging Bull run coming in the midst of 2024, so are you ready to be a **crypto millionaire!!**

If you are one of those who wants to make it big and have a long Bucket List of dreams and things to do before its too late, then lets go straight to where the action is, "THE ABC's OF CRYPTO" ......

TABLE OF CONTENTS

CHAPTER 1:

Understanding the Crypto Landscape. 4

The Rise of Cryptocurrencies Blockchain Technology: An Introduction. 4

Some Prominent types of Cryptocurrencies 8

Benefits and Risks of Investing in Cryptocurrencies 16
CHAPTER 2:
Developing the Millionaire Mindset
19
Adopting a Growth Mindset for Success   19
Overcoming Fear and Risk Aversion -MILLIONAIRE MINDSET 21
Building Resilience in the Face of Market Volatility 24
Diversify Your Portfolio, Cultivating Patience ,and Long-Term Thinking 24
Embracing Volatility, Cultivating Patience and Long-Term Thinking 26

CHAPTER 3:
Identifying Lucrative Investment Opportunities: 29

Researching Promising Cryptocurrencies   32
Understanding the Market Landscape: 32
Identifying Promising Projects: 32
Conducting In-Depth Research: 33
Recap on the Fundamentals of a Cryptocurrency 36
Assessing the Potential for Growth and Adoption 38
Setting Clear Investment Goals 40

Chapter 4:
Building a Solid   Investment Strategy 42
Spreading Risks for Long-Term Success 44
Creating a Balanced Portfolio 48
Implementing Risk Management Strategies 50
CASE STUDY: CHINA AND THE CRYPTO CURRENCIES BAN 53
Chapter 5:
The Future and Cryptocurrency Market -55
Understanding the Bull and Bear Markets: 56
Identifying Market Manipulation and Scams 59
WHAT IS BITCOIN ETF's: 60
Current Market situation: 63
The past: SEC stance, The present: Shift in SEC's position and the Road

ahead:

CHAPTER 6 :

THE FINAL STEPS TOWARDS YOUR MILLIONAIRE MINDSET 66

GETTING STARTED IN CRYPTO WORLD: THE PROCESS ...67

FINAL SUMMARY 69

Chapter 1: Understanding the Crypto Landscape

The Rise of Cryptocurrencies

In recent years, cryptocurrencies have taken the financial world by storm, revolutionizing the way we transact and invest. This chapter will delve into the remarkable rise of cryptocurrencies and how they have become an enticing investment opportunity for business owners.

Cryptocurrencies, such as Bitcoin, Ethereum, ADA, Solana, or Ripple, and many other coins have gained significant popularity due to their decentralized nature and the potential for high returns on investment. Unlike traditional currencies, cryptocurrencies operate on a technology called block chain, which ensures transparency, security, and immutability of transactions. This has given rise to a whole new digital economy, offering exciting opportunities for business owners to diversify their investment portfolios.

One of the key factors contributing to the rise of cryptocurrencies is their independence from traditional financial institutions. Business owners, who often face numerous hurdles when dealing with banks and other intermediaries, are now drawn to the decentralized nature of cryptocurrencies. With cryptocurrencies, business owners have greater control over their financial transactions and can minimize the costs associated with traditional banking.

Another driving force behind the rise of cryptocurrencies is the potential for substantial financial gains. Many early adopters of cryptocurrencies, known as **"crypto bloomers,"** have amassed substantial wealth by investing in these digital assets. This has sparked a frenzy of interest among business owners, who are eager to explore this new investment avenue and potentially achieve similar financial success.

Additionally, the rise of cryptocurrencies has been fueled by the growing acceptance of digital currencies in various industries. Major companies, including Microsoft, PayPal, and Tesla, have started accepting cryptocurrencies as a form of payment, further legitimizing their use and increasing their value. This adoption by mainstream businesses has opened up a world of opportunities for business owners to integrate cryptocurrencies into their own operations and attract a broader customer base.

However, it is crucial for each of us to approach cryptocurrency investments with a strategic mindset. While the potential for high returns exists, the market can be highly volatile and unpredictable. Therefore, it is essential to conduct thorough research, seek expert advice, and devise a well-informed investment strategy to minimize risks and maximize potential gains, which is attempted in this book, This book can serve the beginners and the professionals as its a STEP BY STEP process explained in later half of the book.

QUOTE: **I think bitcoin is on the verge of getting broad acceptance by conventional finance people.- Elon Musk.**

In conclusion, the rise of cryptocurrencies has presented investors with a unique investment opportunity. With their decentralized nature, potential for financial gains, and increasing acceptance in various industries, cryptocurrencies have become an attractive option for diversifying investment portfolios. However, caution and a well-defined investment strategy are necessary to navigate the volatile cryptocurrency market successfully. By adopting a **crypto millionaire** mindset and seizing the opportunities presented by cryptocurrencies, Anyone can position themselves to thrive in this digital economy.

QUOTE: "Riding the crypto wave can ensure you have a chance to embrace the future of money "- Deepak Chandray

Blockchain Technology: An Introduction.

In today's digital age, blockchain technology has emerged as a game-changer, revolutionizing various industries, including finance, supply chain management, healthcare, and more. Understanding the basics of blockchain technology is crucial, especially when it comes to exploring cryptocurrency investment opportunities. This chapter aims to provide you with a concise yet comprehensive overview of this revolutionary technology.

At its core, blockchain is a decentralized, distributed ledger that records and verifies transactions across multiple computers or nodes. Unlike traditional centralized systems, where a single entity has control over the data, blockchain operates on a peer-to-peer network, ensuring transparency, security, and immutability.

One of the key features of blockchain technology is its ability to create digital assets called cryptocurrencies. Cryptocurrencies utilize blockchain as a means of enabling secure, peer-to-peer transactions without the need for intermediaries like banks or governments.

Blockchain technology also introduces the concept of smart contracts. These are self-executing contracts with predefined rules and conditions, stored on the block chain. Smart contracts eliminate the need for intermediaries, reduce costs, and increase efficiency in various business processes.

It is essential to recognize the potential impact of block chain technology on your industry. By embracing this technology, you can streamline operations, enhance security, and explore new business models. Additionally, investing in cryptocurrencies can provide you with an opportunity to diversify your investment portfolio and potentially achieve significant returns.

However, it is crucial to approach cryptocurrency investments with caution. The market is highly volatile, and thorough research and risk management strategies are necessary. Do consider seeking professional advice to make informed investment decisions.

In conclusion, By grasping the basics of block chain, you can unlock immense potential for growth and innovation in your business or embrace the **crypto millionaire** mindset, or explore the possibilities, and embark on a journey towards financial success.

QUOTE : "Anything that can conceive of as a supply chain, blockchain can vastly improve its efficiency- it doesn't matter if its people, numbers, data, money. — Ginni Rometty", CEO of IBM.

Some Prominent types of Cryptocurrencies

In today's digital age, cryptocurrencies have emerged as a revolutionary form of investment, attracting the attention of all classes of people. This chapter will explore some of the Major 6-7 types of cryptocurrencies,

1. Bitcoin (BTC): Bitcoin, the pioneer of cryptocurrencies, remains the most well-known and widely used digital currency. As a decentralized currency, Bitcoin operates on a peer-to-peer network without the need for intermediaries like banks,making it an attractive investment option for business owners looking for long-term growth.

QUOTE" Bitcoin is a technological tour de force".
— Bill Gates

2. Ethereum (ETH): Ethereum is not just a cryptocurrency but also a decentralized platform that enables the development of smart contracts and decentralized applications (DApps). The cryptocurrency associated with Ethereum is called Ether. With its focus on enabling programmable money and innovation.

3. Ripple (XRP): Ripple is a unique cryptocurrency that aims to revolutionize the banking industry. Unlike Bitcoin and Ethereum, Ripple focuses on providing fast, low-cost international money transfers. This makes Ripple an appealing choice for business owners engaged in global transactions, as it can significantly reduce transaction costs and processing times.

4.SOLANA (SOL): Solana launched in March 2020, is a high performance permissionless blockchain using the Proof of Stake (Pos) consensus algorithm with the Proof-of- History(PoH) mechanism to facilitate and verify transactions.It is a smart contract blockchain network that allows to deploy decentralised applications and launch fungible and non fungible tokens(NFTs). in Few years since its launch, the solana Network has become a hotbed for NFT activity, New token and dApp launches, and more.

5.Cardano (ADA): Cardano is a blockchain platform that aims to provide a secure and scalable infrastructure for the development of decentralized applications and smart contracts. Its cryptocurrency, ADA, powers the Cardano network. Business owners seeking to invest in the potential of blockchain technology and its applications can explore the opportunities presented by Cardano.

6.CHAINLINK(LINK): Chainlink is a decentralised oracle network built on Ethereum, feeding real-world data from external sources to smart contracts and supported blockchain platforms. The Chainlink network enables users to connect smart contracts to decentralized trusted notes serving available data collected from external sources and APIs.

7.POLKADOT: Polkadot is a blockchain project that was founded in 2016 and launched its mainnet in 2020. Polkadot founded by Gavin Wood, an English computer scientist that was also one of the founding members of the Ethereum project. Polkadot allows parachains, which are customizable blockchains built using the Substrate framework, to interoperate with each other. Developers can tailor the features of their parachain to their specific needs, while still inheriting the security of the Relay Chain, which is at the core of the Polkadot network.

These are just a few examples of the diverse range of cryptocurrencies available for investment. Each cryptocurrency has its own unique features, use cases, and potential returns. As a business owner, it is essential to conduct thorough research, seek expert advice, and stay updated with market trends to make informed investment decisions.

QUOTE: "If you don't believe it or don't get it, I don't have the time to try to convince you, sorry". - Satoshi Nakamoto, founder of Bitcoin.

Remember, the world of cryptocurrencies is constantly evolving, and new cryptocurrencies are introduced regularly. By staying knowledgeable and open-minded, business owners can position themselves to capitalize on the ever-expanding cryptocurrency investment opportunities and potentially unlock immense financial gains, here is a quick study to know how well versed you are in the crypto world.

Questions for your crypto millionaire journey.

1. In what year were you born?

A)GenZ (born 1997-2003) [18-24]

B)Millennials (born 1981-1996) [25-40]

C)Gen X (born 1965-1980) [41-56]

D)Baby Boomers (born 1946-1964) [57-75]

E)Silent Generation (born 1945 or earlier) [76+]

2.Do you have any technology background?

A)Not at all

B) Yes a bit, Slightly Aware.

C)Professional

3.How do you classify your knowledge about cryptocurrency?

The answer should be a single choice:

1. .Not at all familiar
2. Slightly familiar
3. Moderately familiar
4. Very familiar
5. Extremely familiar

6. Have you ever participated in any cryptocurrency activities? If yes, name them

4.The reason behind you to prefer cryptocurrency over nations currency.

A)Data privacy concern

B)Government permissions and acceptance

C)Low business acceptance

D)Security Issues

E)Physical cash are too strong to handle

5. In your opinion, does an open source digital currency where no dedicated intermediary organisation or sovereign government controls apply, present relatively a greater or lesser risk as an asset in a portfolio or treasury account compared with other currency holdings? Select one.

A)great risk

B)Somewhat greater risk

C)Neither greater nor lesser risk

D)Somewhat lesser risk

E)Much lesser risk

6.In your opinion, should open source digital currencies (cryptocurrencies such as Bitcoin, Ethereum,ADA,SOLANA,XRP.. etc) be considered strictly as a currency for settling transactions or as an asset for storing/appreciating value? Select one.

A)An open source digital currency should be treated as a regular currency such as dollars, euros or yen

B)An open source digital currency should be treated as an asset like gold, property or other commodity

C)An open source digital currency should be treated as both a currency for transactions and an asset for storing/appreciating value

D)An open source digital currency should be treated neither as a currency for transactions nor an asset for storing/appreciating value

7.In your opinion, what would trigger more portfolio/treasury activity in open source digital currencies (cryptocurrencies such as but not limited to Bitcoin)?

The answer could be a multiple choice:

A)Wider adoption/acceptance of central bank digital currencies (CBDCs)

B)Availability of an institutional-only digital currency exchange platform

C)Increased economic instability

D)More robust anti-money laundering (AML) controls for digital currencies

E)Significant purchase/support of digital currencies by leading corporations

F)A sharp rise in other asset prices such as gold and/or equities

G)A sharp fall in other asset prices such as gold and/or equities Reductions in the purchasing power of my country's fiat currency

H)New regulatory framework from government

I)Rising interest rates

J)Continued low/negative interest rates

Benefits and Risks of Investing in Cryptocurrencies

Cryptocurrencies have taken the financial world by storm, offering business owners unique investment opportunities. However, before diving headfirst into this exciting and volatile market, it is essential to understand the benefits and risks associated with investing in cryptocurrencies.

One of the most significant advantages of investing in cryptocurrencies is the potential for high returns. Unlike traditional investments such as stocks or real estate, where the returns are often gradual and predictable, cryptocurrencies offer the possibility of exponential growth. Some early investors in Bitcoin and other cryptocurrencies have become millionaires, making it an attractive investment option for business owners seeking substantial profits.

Another benefit of investing in cryptocurrencies is the decentralization of the market. Unlike traditional financial systems controlled by banks or governments, cryptocurrencies operate on a decentralized network, making transactions more secure and transparent. Additionally, cryptocurrencies provide an alternative to traditional banking systems, enabling business owners to conduct international transactions quickly and at a lower cost.

Furthermore, investing in cryptocurrencies allows business owners to diversify their investment portfolios. By allocating a portion of their funds to cryptocurrencies, entrepreneurs can spread their risk and potentially benefit from the growth of this emerging market. Diversification is crucial in mitigating the impact of market volatility and can provide a hedge against inflation and economic uncertainty.

However, it is vital to recognize the risks associated with investing in cryptocurrencies. One of the primary risks is the market's extreme volatility. Cryptocurrency prices can fluctuate dramatically within a short period, leading to substantial losses if not properly managed. Therefore, business owners must exercise caution and conduct thorough research before investing in any particular cryptocurrency.

Another significant risk is the potential for fraud and hacking. Since cryptocurrencies operate in a digital realm, they are vulnerable to cyber attacks and scams. Business owners must take necessary precautions to protect their digital assets, such as using secure wallets and employing robust cybersecurity measures.

Regulatory and legal agencies have slowly embraced the cryptocurrency investments in ETFs. US regulators like the SEC have approved the application for 11 investment funds like Blackrock, Invesco, Fidelity, Ark Investments and others for BITCOIN ETF and the sudden rush by various Investment funds for ETFs in crypto currencies is increasing on a daily basis.

In conclusion, investing in cryptocurrencies offers business owners unique opportunities for high returns, diversification, and decentralized transactions. However, it is essential to recognize and manage the associated risks, such as market volatility, fraud, and regulatory uncertainties. By understanding these benefits and risks, business owners can make informed decisions.

Chapter 2: Developing the Millionaire Mindset

Adopting a Growth Mindset for Success

In the fast-paced world of cryptocurrency investment opportunities, success is not solely determined by knowledge and expertise in the field. It is equally crucial to cultivate a growth mindset that can propel you towards achieving your financial goals. A growth mindset allows business owners to embrace challenges, persist through setbacks, and continuously adapt and learn from experiences.

As a business owner venturing into the world of cryptocurrency investment, it is important to understand that setbacks and market volatility are inevitable. Instead of viewing them as failures, one should perceive them as valuable learning experiences that contribute to personal and professional growth.

To foster a growth mindset, it is imperative to develop a passion for learning. Stay abreast of the latest trends, technological advancements, and market dynamics in the cryptocurrency industry. Continuously seek out educational resources such as books, articles, and podcasts to expand your knowledge base. Attend conferences and engage in networking opportunities to connect with industry experts and gain insights from their experiences.

Embracing a growth mindset also entails stepping out of your comfort zone. Take calculated risks and challenge yourself to explore new investment opportunities. Be open to trying different strategies and approaches, even if they may initially seem daunting or unfamiliar. Remember, growth and success often lie just beyond the boundaries of your comfort zone.

In conclusion, adopting a growth mindset is crucial for success in the dynamic world of cryptocurrency investment. By embracing challenges, staying curious and open to learning, maintaining a positive outlook, stepping out of your comfort zone, and engaging in self-reflection, you can unlock your full potential as a business owner in the cryptocurrency space. Embrace the growth mindset and pave your way towards becoming a **crypto millionaire.**

Millionaire Mindset

Overcoming Fear and Risk Aversion

In the world of business, fear and risk aversion can be major roadblocks to success. This is particularly true when it comes to exploring new investment opportunities, such as cryptocurrency. As a business owner, it is crucial to overcome these barriers and develop a mindset that embraces calculated risks. In this chapter, we will discuss how to overcome fear and risk aversion, specifically in the context of cryptocurrency investment opportunities.

Fear of the unknown is a common reason why many business owners shy away from exploring cryptocurrency investments. However, it is important to remember that any successful business venture involves some level of risk. By educating yourself about cryptocurrency and understanding its potential benefits, you can alleviate some of these fears. Engage in thorough research, attend industry conferences, and connect with experts in the field to expand your knowledge and gain confidence in your decision-making.

Another aspect of overcoming fear is acknowledging that failure is a valuable learning experience. Cryptocurrency investments may not always yield immediate results, and setbacks are inevitable. Embrace these setbacks as opportunities for growth and learning, and use them to refine your investment strategies. By adopting a growth mindset, you can transform fear into motivation and ensure that setbacks do not deter you from exploring the vast potential of cryptocurrency investments.

Risk aversion can also hinder business owners from venturing into cryptocurrency investments. It is crucial to understand that not taking risks can be just as detrimental as taking unwarranted risks. Cryptocurrency investment opportunities have the potential for high returns, but they also come with volatility and uncertainty. By diversifying your investment portfolio and carefully analyzing market trends, you can mitigate risks and make informed decisions. It is essential to strike a balance between risk and reward, and embracing calculated risks can lead to substantial financial gains.

To overcome fear and risk aversion, it is vital to surround yourself with like-minded individuals who have successfully navigated the cryptocurrency investment landscape. Join local or online communities that focus on cryptocurrency investments and engage in discussions to gain insights and learn from their experiences. Additionally, consider seeking guidance from financial advisors or professionals with expertise in cryptocurrency investments. Their knowledge and expertise can help you navigate the complexities of this market and alleviate any fears or doubts you may have.

Remember, overcoming fear and risk aversion is crucial for business owners looking to capitalize on the tremendous potential of cryptocurrency investments. By expanding your knowledge, embracing calculated risks, and surrounding yourself with the right support network, you can develop the mindset of a crypto millionaire and unlock a world of financial opportunities.

Building Resilience in the Face of Market Volatility

As a business owner, navigating the world of cryptocurrency investments can be both exciting and challenging. The volatile nature of the market makes it essential for you to build resilience to withstand the ups and downs that come with investing in this emerging asset class. In this subchapter, we will explore key strategies and mindset shifts that can help you develop the resilience needed to thrive in the face of market volatility.

1. **Diversify Your Portfolio**: One of the fundamental principles of building resilience in cryptocurrency investments is diversification. Rather than putting all your eggs in one basket, consider spreading your investments across different cryptocurrencies and sectors. This strategy helps mitigate risk and reduces the impact of any single investment on your overall portfolio.

2. **Stay Informed**: Knowledge is power in the world of cryptocurrency investments. Stay up-to-date with the latest news, trends, and regulatory changes. By being well-informed, you can make informed decisions that are based on a deep understanding of the market. Consider joining online communities, attending conferences, and subscribing to reputable newsletters to stay ahead of the curve.

3. **Embrace Volatility as an Opportunity**: While market volatility can be intimidating, it also presents opportunities for profit. Rather than fearing volatility, embrace it as a chance to buy low and sell high. Develop a long-term perspective and have faith in the potential of cryptocurrencies.

Remember, successful investors often capitalize on market downturns to accumulate assets at discounted prices.

4. **Set Realistic Expectations**: Cryptocurrency investments can be highly lucrative, but they are not without risks. Set realistic expectations and avoid get-rich-quick mentalities. Understand that the market is subject to sudden fluctuations and that returns may not always be immediate. Patience, perseverance, and a long-term investment horizon are crucial for building resilience in the face of market volatility.

5. **Practice Emotional Discipline**: Emotional discipline is vital when dealing with market volatility. Avoid making impulsive decisions based on fear or greed. Develop a mindset that focuses on the long-term potential rather than short-term fluctuations. Consider setting predefined exit points and sticking to your investment strategy, irrespective of market sentiment.

Building resilience in the face of market volatility is a continuous process that requires dedication and adaptability. By diversifying your portfolio, staying informed, embracing volatility, setting realistic expectations, and practicing emotional discipline, you can fortify your mindset and significantly increase your chances of success in cryptocurrency investments.

Remember, the key to becoming a crypto millionaire lies not only in financial acumen but also in developing the right mindset to weather the storms and seize the opportunities that come your way.

Cultivating Patience and Long-Term Thinking

In the fast-paced world of cryptocurrency investment opportunities, cultivating patience and long-term thinking is crucial for business owners looking to succeed. This chapter aims to provide valuable insights and strategies to help you develop the mindset of a **crypto millionaire**.

One of the most common mistakes made by novice investors is the tendency to focus on short-term gains. While it is true that cryptocurrency markets can be highly volatile, successful business owners understand the importance of looking beyond daily fluctuations and focusing on long-term goals.

Patience is a virtue in the world of cryptocurrency investment. It is essential to resist the temptation to make impulsive decisions based on short-term market trends. Instead, take the time to thoroughly research and evaluate potential investments, considering factors such as the project's fundamentals, team, and long-term growth potential.

Another aspect of cultivating patience is understanding that cryptocurrency markets go through cycles. There will be periods of rapid growth and bullish trends, followed by periods of consolidation or even decline. By embracing these cycles and adopting a long-term perspective, you can make more informed investment decisions.

Long-term thinking is about understanding the potential of cryptocurrency beyond its current state. As a business owner, you already possess the visionary mindset required to identify trends and opportunities. Apply this mindset to the world of cryptocurrency investment, envisioning the potential impact of block chain technology on various industries and the global economy.

To develop a long-term mindset, it is crucial to stay informed and educated about the latest developments in the cryptocurrency space. Attend conferences, join forums, and engage with industry experts to gain insights and knowledge. This continuous learning journey will help you identify emerging trends and make informed decisions about your investments.

Furthermore, successful business owners understand the importance of diversification. While cryptocurrency investment can be highly profitable, it also carries inherent risks. Diversifying your portfolio across different cryptocurrencies and even other asset classes can help mitigate these risks and ensure a more stable long-term investment strategy.

In conclusion, cultivating patience and long-term thinking is essential for business owners looking to capitalize on cryptocurrency investment opportunities. By embracing patience, resisting short-term trends, and adopting a long-term mindset, you can make more informed investment decisions that maximize your chances of achieving the crypto millionaire status. Remember to stay informed, diversify your portfolio, and always keep your long-term goals in mind.

QUESTIONS TO PONDER:

1. WOULD YOU LIKE TO BE A MILLIONAIRE BY INVESTING IN CRYPTO CURRENCIES?

YES□ NO□

2.AS INFORMED ABOVE WOULD YOU LIKE TO INVEST IN THE TOP 5 OR 6 CRYPTOS.

YES □ NO□

3.ARE YOU A LONG TERM INVESTOR?

YES □ NO□

4.ARE YOU LOOKING FOR SHORT TERM GAINS LIKE 3-6 MONTHS

YES NO□

5.CAN YOU LOOK AT YOUR INVESTMENTS PARKED IN CRYPTOCURRENCIES FOR A HORIZON OF 3-5 YEARS:

YES □ NO□

6.WHICH CRYPTO CURRENCIES AMONG THE ABOVE INTERESTS YOU

(Name them on a scale from 1 to 7)

BITCOIN (BTC) □

ETHEREUM(ETH) □

SOLANA (SOL) ☐

CARDANO(ADA) ☐

RIPPLE (XRP) ☐

POLKADOT(DOT) ☐

1. WHICH OF THESE WOULD YOU LIKE TO BE IN YOUR
   PORTFOLIO OF DIVERSIFIED ASSETS? WRITE THEM BELOW
   FOR YOUR INVESTMENT PLANS.

Researching Promising Cryptocurrencies

In the fast-paced world of cryptocurrency, staying ahead of the curve is crucial for business owners seeking to capitalize on investment opportunities. Researching promising cryptocurrencies is an essential step towards building a successful crypto portfolio that can potentially lead to substantial wealth accumulation. This subchapter delves into the strategies and techniques that business owners can employ to identify and evaluate potential crypto investments.

Understanding the Market Landscape:

To begin your cryptocurrency research journey, it is imperative to gain a deep understanding of the market landscape. This involves studying the various types of cryptocurrencies, their underlying technologies, and the unique features that differentiate them. Familiarize yourself with terms such as blockchain, decentralized finance (DeFi), and smart contracts, as they form the foundation of many promising cryptocurrencies.

Identifying Promising Projects:

Focus on identifying promising projects within the cryptocurrency space. Look for cryptocurrencies that offer innovative solutions to real-world problems, have a strong development team, and a growing community of supporters. Consider factors such as market demand, scalability, and regulatory compliance, as these can greatly impact the long-term success of a cryptocurrency.

Conducting In-Depth Research:

When researching specific cryptocurrencies, it is crucial to conduct thorough due diligence. Analyze the project's whitepaper, roadmap, and technical documentation to gain insights into its goals, functionality, and potential challenges. Examine the team's background, previous achievements, and their level of transparency.

Staying Updated:

Cryptocurrency markets are highly volatile, and new projects emerge frequently. To stay ahead, it is essential to stay updated with the latest news, market trends, and regulatory developments. Follow reputable cryptocurrency news platforms, join relevant forums and communities, and engage in discussions with industry experts. This will enable you to make informed decisions based on the most up-to-date information.

Seeking Professional Advice:
It can be beneficial to seek professional advice when researching promising cryptocurrencies. Consult with experts who specialize in cryptocurrency investments and have a proven track record of success. Their expertise and insights can help you navigate the complexities of the market and make informed investment decisions.

In conclusion, researching promising cryptocurrencies is a crucial step for YOU, who is looking to explore investment opportunities in the cryptocurrency space. By understanding the market landscape, identifying promising projects, conducting thorough research, staying updated, and seeking professional advice. Remember, thorough research is the key to unlocking the door to successful crypto investments and building a *millionaire mindset* in the world of cryptocurrency.

Analyzing Market Trends and Patterns

In the ever-evolving world of cryptocurrency investment opportunities, understanding market trends and patterns is crucial for looking into capitalizing in this emerging market. The ability to analyze and interpret these trends can help you make informed investment decisions, mitigate risks, and ultimately pave the way towards becoming a crypto millionaire.

This chapter will delve into the various tools and techniques used to analyze market trends and patterns in the cryptocurrency space. Whether you are a seasoned investor or just starting your journey, this knowledge will provide you with a competitive edge and increase your chances of success.

One of the key aspects of analyzing market trends is understanding market cycles. Cryptocurrency markets are highly volatile and often experience distinct cycles of bull and bear markets. By studying historical data, you can identify patterns and predict potential market movements. We will explore the different stages of these cycles and provide insights on how to navigate them effectively.

Technical analysis is another essential tool in analyzing market trends and patterns. This method involves studying historical price and volume data to predict future price movements. We will discuss various technical indicators, chart patterns, and trend lines that can assist you in making informed investment decisions. Understanding support and resistance levels, moving averages, and other technical analysis tools will enable you to identify entry and exit points for your crypto investments.

Moreover, fundamental analysis plays a significant role in evaluating the potential of cryptocurrencies. By examining factors such as project team, technology, market demand, and regulatory environment, you can determine the long-term viability and growth prospects of a cryptocurrency. We will provide you with a comprehensive framework to conduct fundamental analysis and identify promising investment opportunities.

In addition to these analytical techniques, we will also discuss the importance of staying updated with market news, industry trends, and regulatory developments. Being aware of the latest happenings in the cryptocurrency space can give you valuable insights into market sentiment and help you make timely investment decisions.

By mastering the art of analyzing market trends and patterns, business owners can position themselves for success in the world of cryptocurrency investments. This subchapter will equip you with the necessary knowledge and tools to navigate this dynamic market with confidence, allowing you to unlock the potential of crypto assets and achieve the coveted millionaire mindset.

Recap on the Fundamentals of a Cryptocurrency

Cryptocurrency investment opportunities have gained significant attention in recent years, attracting business owners looking to diversify their investment portfolios and capitalize on the potential of this new digital asset class. However, before diving into the exciting world of cryptocurrencies, it is crucial for business owners to evaluate the fundamentals of each cryptocurrency to make informed investment decisions. This subchapter aims to provide a comprehensive guide on how to evaluate the fundamentals of a cryptocurrency.

When evaluating the fundamentals of a cryptocurrency, it is essential to consider factors such as the technology behind it, the team behind the project, the market demand, and its potential for long-term growth. Firstly, understanding the underlying technology, such as blockchain, is crucial. A robust and innovative technology can determine the scalability, security, and efficiency of the cryptocurrency, making it more likely to succeed in the long run.

Additionally, evaluating the team behind the cryptocurrency project is **essential and important**. A competent and experienced team can provide the necessary expertise to drive the project forward and overcome potential challenges. Researching the team's background, track record, and their level of commitment to the project is crucial in determining the legitimacy and potential success of the cryptocurrency.

Furthermore, assessing the market demand for a particular cryptocurrency is vital. Understanding the problem it aims to solve and whether there is a real need for its implementation can help determine its potential for adoption and future growth. It is also important to consider the competitive landscape and whether the cryptocurrency has a unique value proposition that sets it apart from existing alternatives.

Finally, analyzing the potential for long-term growth is crucial for business owners. This involves studying the cryptocurrency's roadmap, future developments, and partnerships. Additionally, keeping an eye on regulatory developments and industry trends can help assess the risks and opportunities associated with a specific cryptocurrency.

In conclusion, evaluating the fundamentals of a cryptocurrency is of utmost importance for business owners looking to venture into the world of cryptocurrency investments. By understanding the technology, assessing the team behind the project, analyzing market demand, and considering long-term growth potential, business owners can make informed decisions and increase their chances of success in this rapidly evolving market.

Assessing the Potential for Growth and Adoption

In the ever-evolving world of cryptocurrencies, opportunities for investment abound. As a business owner, it is crucial to stay ahead of the curve and explore the potential for growth and adoption in this exciting market. This subchapter will delve into the key factors to consider when assessing the potential for growth and adoption in cryptocurrency investment opportunities.

One of the primary factors to evaluate is the market demand for a particular cryptocurrency. Is there a clear need or problem that this digital asset aims to solve? Understanding the underlying technology and its real-world applications can give you valuable insights into its growth potential. Additionally, consider the size of the target market and the projected growth rate. Is there a significant user base that can fuel the adoption of this cryptocurrency? Assessing these factors will help you gauge the potential for future returns on your investment.

Furthermore, it is essential to evaluate the team behind the cryptocurrency project. Look into the qualifications and experience of the core team members. Have they successfully executed similar projects in the past? A competent team with a proven track record can significantly enhance the likelihood of a cryptocurrency's success. Additionally, examine the partnerships and collaborations that the project has established. Strong partnerships can provide credibility and open doors to wider adoption.

Regulatory considerations should also be taken into account. Cryptocurrencies operate in a relatively nascent and evolving regulatory landscape. Assess the legal and regulatory frameworks surrounding the cryptocurrency you are considering investing in. Understand the level of regulatory scrutiny and potential risks associated with compliance. A thorough analysis of the regulatory environment can help you navigate potential obstacles and ensure a smooth investment journey.

Lastly, stay informed about the broader market trends and sentiments. Keep a close eye on news and developments within the cryptocurrency industry as well as the global financial sector. Understanding market dynamics and investor sentiment will help you make informed investment decisions. Keep in mind that the cryptocurrency market is highly volatile, so it is crucial to balance risk and reward.

Assessing the potential for growth and adoption in cryptocurrency investment opportunities requires careful analysis and consideration. By evaluating market demand, the team behind the project, regulatory factors, and broader market trends, you can make informed investment decisions that align with your business goals. Remember, the crypto millionaire mindset is built on knowledge, strategy, and taking calculated risks.

Setting Clear Investment Goals

One of the most crucial steps in achieving success in cryptocurrency investment opportunities is setting clear investment goals. we are no strangers to goal-setting and the same applies to our investments in the crypto market.

Why is setting clear investment goals so vital? Without a defined objective, it becomes challenging to make informed decisions and stay focused on your investment strategy. Setting clear goals helps provide direction, motivation, and a sense of purpose to your investment journey.

The first step in setting investment goals is to assess your financial situation and determine how much capital you are willing to allocate to cryptocurrency investments. Consider factors such as your risk tolerance, liquidity requirements, and overall investment portfolio diversification. This assessment will help you set realistic expectations and avoid overextending yourself financially.

Please write your goals: $1000-5000, $5000-20000,$20000-50000 per year, or higher as per your risk appetite for 3-5years.

Chapter 4: Building a Solid Investment Strategy

SPENDING MONEY LIKE A MILLIONAIRE

Brokenaires		Millionaires	
Clothes	$200	Investments	$300
Shoes	$100	Groceries	$300
Restaurants	$350	Gym Membership	$80
Drinks	$200	Courses	$100
Uber	$150	Books	$50
Streaming	$100	Rental Fund	$250
Vapes	$80	Seminars	$100
Total	$1,180	Total	$1,180
R.O.I.	$NONE	R.O.I.	$INFINITE

MasteringWealth

Source: Mastering wealth.

Identify yourself, make the changes, you are most likely an average of what your nearest friends or associates are:
Rich people associate with positive, successful people, Poor people associate with negative or unsuccessful people.
Rich people manage their money well. Poor people mismanage their money well.

Rich people think big. Poor people think small.
Rich people focus on opportunities. Poor people focus on obstacles.

It is essential to define your investment time horizon. Are you looking for short-term gains or long-term wealth accumulation? Cryptocurrency markets can be highly volatile, so your time horizon will determine your returns, be a long term investor.

TIME FRAME: 1-3, 3-5, 5-10 years minimum. These investments are liquid and can be liquidated for any emergencies, read the exchange terms before investing.

Once you have established your financial capacity and time horizon, narrow down your investment goals to per month basis. Clearly outlining your objectives will help you choose the right cryptocurrencies and investment vehicles that align with your goals.

Finally, revisit and reassess your investment goals periodically. As the cryptocurrency market evolves, your goals may need to be adjusted to adapt to the changing landscape. Regularly reviewing and redefining your objectives will ensure that your investment strategy remains aligned with your financial aspirations.

In conclusion, setting clear investment goals is a fundamental aspect of achieving success in cryptocurrency investments. we understand the importance of goal-setting in our jobs or business, and the same principles apply to our investments. By assessing our financial situation, defining our investment time horizon, narrowing down our objectives, considering our risk appetite, and periodically reviewing our goals, we can establish a solid foundation for our cryptocurrency investment journey.

Diversification: Spreading Risks for Long-Term Success

In the world of cryptocurrency investment opportunities, diversification plays a crucial role in ensuring long-term success and mitigating risks. As a business owner interested in venturing into the realm of crypto investments, understanding the importance of diversification can significantly impact your journey towards becoming a crypto millionaire.

Diversification refers to the practice of spreading your investments across different assets, sectors, or industries. Instead of putting all your eggs in one basket, diversifying your crypto portfolio allows you to minimize the potential impact of a single investment going awry. By distributing your investments, you create a safety net that protects you from any unforeseen circumstances or market fluctuations.

The cryptocurrency market is known for its volatility, making diversification even more critical. While some cryptocurrencies may experience rapid growth, others may suffer significant losses. By diversifying, you can balance out the risks and rewards of your investments, ensuring that any potential losses from one asset are offset by gains from another.

One approach to diversification is investing in cryptocurrencies with different underlying technologies or use cases. For example, you could allocate a portion of your portfolio to established cryptocurrencies like Bitcoin or Ethereum, while also exploring promising altcoins or tokens that are based on innovative technologies such as blockchain or decentralized finance (DeFi).

Additionally, diversifying across different sectors within the crypto industry can also be beneficial. Cryptocurrencies have expanded beyond just digital currencies; they now encompass various sectors like decentralized applications (dApps), non-fungible tokens (NFTs), and even the emerging metaverse. By investing in a range of sectors, you tap into different growth opportunities while reducing your exposure to any single sector's risks.

Market Cap$1 to $1T

Crypto /   Name / Tech Adoption Grade/ Market Performance Grade/
Price
Rating

			Tech Adoption Grade	Market Performance Grade
A	Bitcoin	BTC	A	B+
	$43,841.91			
B	Ethereum	ETH	B+	B+
	$2,384.47			
B	Solana	SOL	B	A-
	$106.26			
B	Ripple	XRP	B-	C+
	$0.525296			
C	BNB	BNB	C+	B-
	$309.81			
B	Cardano	ADA	B-	B+
	$0.520945			
B	Celestia	TIA	B	A
	$18.43			
B	Avalanche	AVAX	B+	A-
	$36.42			
A	ChainLink	LINK	B+	A-
	$15.67			
C	Dogecoin	DOGE	B-	D+
	$0.081690			
C	OKB	OKB	D+	B-
	$53.28			
C	TRON	TRX	C-	B+
	$0.113326			
B	Polkadot	DOT	B-	B
	$7.04			
B	Polygon	MATIC	B+	C+
	$0.819606			

Source: weiss ratings. Please visit weiss ratings for more in depth analysis on the crypto currencies.

However, it's important to note that diversification does not guarantee profits or eliminate all risks. It is crucial to conduct thorough research, stay updated with market trends, and seek advice from reputable sources before making any investment decisions.

In conclusion, diversification is a key strategy for business owners looking to navigate the cryptocurrency investment landscape successfully. By spreading your risks across different assets and sectors, you increase your chances of long-term success while safeguarding your investments against potential market downturns. Remember, the path to becoming a crypto millionaire lies not in putting all your eggs in one basket but in diversifying your crypto portfolio wisely.

Creating a Balanced Portfolio

In the fast-paced and ever-evolving world of cryptocurrency investment opportunities, it is crucial for business owners to have a balanced portfolio. A balanced portfolio can help mitigate risks and maximize potential returns, ensuring long-term success in this dynamic market. In this subchapter, we will delve into the key strategies and considerations for creating a balanced portfolio that aligns with the Crypto Millionaire Mindset.

Diversification is the cornerstone of a balanced portfolio. By spreading your investments across different cryptocurrency assets, you can minimize the impact of any single investment's volatility. This means that even if one cryptocurrency underperforms, others in your portfolio may thrive, offsetting potential losses. As a business owner, it is important to apply the same principles of diversification to your cryptocurrency investments as you would to your business ventures.

To achieve diversification, you should consider investing in a mix of established cryptocurrencies and promising emerging ones. Established cryptocurrencies like Bitcoin and Ethereum offer stability and liquidity, making them a solid foundation for your portfolio. However, it is also essential to explore emerging cryptocurrencies that have the potential for exponential growth. These can provide high returns, but they also carry higher risks. By diversifying across different types of cryptocurrencies, you can strike a balance between stability and growth.

Furthermore, it is important to consider the market capitalization of the cryptocurrencies you choose to invest in. Market capitalization reflects the total value of a cryptocurrency and can be a useful indicator of its potential. Investing in a range of cryptocurrencies with varying market capitalizations can help you capture different segments of the market, thus enhancing your portfolio's diversification.

Additionally, one should keep in mind the importance of risk management when creating a balanced portfolio. While cryptocurrency investments offer immense potential, they also come with inherent risks. Setting realistic investment goals, defining acceptable risk levels, and establishing stop-loss orders can help protect your portfolio from extreme volatility and unexpected market downturns.

In conclusion, creating a balanced portfolio is essential for each of us seeking to capitalize on cryptocurrency investment opportunities. By diversifying across different cryptocurrencies, including established and emerging ones, and considering market capitalization, business owners can strike a balance between stability and growth. Remember to implement risk management strategies to protect your portfolio from potential losses. With the Crypto Millionaire Mindset, you can navigate the world of cryptocurrency investments with confidence and make informed decisions that lead to long-term success.

QUOTE: "Bitcoin is a remarkable cryptographic achievement... The ability to create something which is not duplicable in the digital world has enormous value... Lots of people will build businesses on top of that." — Eric Schmidt, Executive Chairman of Google

Implementing Risk Management Strategies

Among the Clutter and the loud noise, it is crucial for business owners to have a solid understanding of risk management strategies. As the market can be highly volatile and unpredictable, it is imperative to take proactive steps to protect your investments and maximize your chances of success. This chapter will guide you through the essential risk management strategies

1.Diversify your portfolio:

One of the fundamental principles of risk management is diversification. By spreading your investments across different cryptocurrencies, you reduce the impact of any single asset's poor performance. This strategy allows you to mitigate potential losses and optimize your chances of capitalizing on profitable opportunities.

2.Set clear investment goals:
Before entering the crypto market, it is essential to define your investment goals. Establishing realistic and measurable objectives will guide your decision-making process and help you stay focused on your long-term strategy. By having a clear vision, you will be less likely to make impulsive decisions driven by market fluctuations.

3.*Conduct some research*
Knowledge is power in the crypto world. To minimize risks, it is vital to thoroughly research any cryptocurrency you plan to invest in. Analyze its

technology, market trends, team background, and potential risks. Stay updated with news and expert opinions to make informed decisions based on reliable information.

3.Establish stop-loss orders:

Stop-loss orders are crucial risk management tools that automatically sell your cryptocurrency assets if they reach a predetermined price level. By setting stop-loss orders, you can limit your potential losses and protect your investments from sudden market downturns.

4.Stay updated with regulatory changes:

Cryptocurrency markets are subject to evolving regulations. It is crucial for business owners to stay informed about any changes in regulatory frameworks that might impact their investments. Legal compliance is an essential aspect of risk management in this industry.

5. Regularly reassess and adjust your strategy:

The crypto market is dynamic, and your risk management strategy should be as well. Regularly reassess your investment portfolio, review your goals, and adjust your strategy based on market conditions and your risk appetite. Flexibility and adaptability are key to success in this ever-changing landscape.

By implementing these risk management strategies, business owners can navigate the cryptocurrency market with confidence and maximize their chances of success. Remember, investing in cryptocurrencies involves risk, and no strategy can guarantee profits. However, by adopting a disciplined and informed approach, you can minimize potential losses and capitalize on the exciting investment opportunities offered by the crypto world. Lets look into a Case study of cryptocurrency BAN in China.

CASE STUDY: CHINA AND THE CRYPTO CURRENCIES BAN

(Source:REUTERS, JANUARY 25'2024)

Crypto trading and mining has been banned in China since 2021. For example Won a Shanghai based finance sector executive, started moving a bit of his money into cryptocurrencies in early 2023, when he realised that the Chinese economy and its stock markets were on the downhill. Won used bank cards issued by small rural commercial banks to buy cryptocurrencies through grey market dealers, and capped each transaction at 50000Yuan ($6978) to escape scrutiny, He now owns roughly 1 Million yuan worth of cryptocurrencies accounting for almost 50% of his investment portfolio and 40% in chinese equities. His cryptoinvestments are up 50% and the equity has been sinking for the last 3 years. More like Won are using creative ways to own Bitcoin and some other crypto assets that they believe are safer than investing in Equities or the property market in Mainland.

Summary of the study:

While cryptocurrency is banned in Mainland China, Some people are still able to trade crypto assets in exchanges such as OKX and Binance or other over the counter channels. Mainland China investors can also possibly open overseas bank accounts to buy crypto assets. After Hongkong's open endorsement of the digital assets in 2023, some Chinese citizens are using their $50000 annual forex purchase quotas to move money in cryptocurrency in Hongkong. China's economic downturn has made investment on mainland risky or uncertain so people are looking to allocate assets offshore. Recently Hongkong witnesses mainland investors looking for crypto assets as they are starved of this opportunities back home.

Despite the ban Chinese crypto market recorded and estimated $86 Billion in raw transaction volumes between July 2022 to June 2023. We can witness crypto exchange stores sprouting in Hongkong's busy business and shopping streets. These offline shops are lightly regulated. Wong believes Chinese officials are aware of the huge potential and hence their endorsement of crypto trading in Hongkong to hold a pie in the crypto business booming in Financial centres like Singapore or New york. Chainalysis reckons the developments have created speculation that the Chinese government maybe warming to the cryptocurrency and Hongkong maybe the testing ground for these efforts.

Chapter 5: The Future and Cryptocurrency Market

In the fast-paced world of cryptocurrency investment opportunities, understanding market cycles and timing is crucial for business owners looking to capitalize on this emerging asset class.Market cycles refer to the recurring patterns and phases that occur in financial markets, including cryptocurrencies. By identifying these cycles, business owners can anticipate market trends and make informed investment decisions. Understanding market cycles is essential for maximizing profits and minimizing risks. As the Market cycles indicate today, The crypto market is transforming, moving from the fringes of finance to the center of many financial advisors attention. You'll recall that the Securities and Exchange Commission approved 11 spot Bitcoin ETFs run by Wall Street giants like BlackRock, Fidelity, Franklin Templeton, Grayscale, VanEck and others. These institutions will funnel huge amounts of new capital from the world of traditional investors to the world of crypto. (source weiss ratings)

- In 2019, the transition year of the last bull market, investors could have made 183% in Bitcoin, 118% in **Ethereum (ETH, "B+")** and 49% in **Cardano (ADA, "B-")**.
- **640%** in Bitcoin, or **3.5x** more than year-one investors.
- **2,537%** in Ethereum,or **21.5x** more than year-one investors
- **4,998%** in Cadano, or a whopping **102x** more than year-one investors.
- We see the same pattern unfolding in the current cycle. Investors who bought our favorite coins at the beginning of 2023 and sold them before year-end could have made very good money. But all our research tells us that investors starting to invest right now could make much more. - **weiss ratings.**

Timing is another critical aspect of cryptocurrency investment. Knowing when to enter or exit the market can make a significant difference in the returns on investment. By mastering timing, business owners can seize opportunities and avoid potential pitfalls. Business owners will learn to identify the signs of a market trending upward (bull market) or downward (bear market).

Understanding these market phases enables business owners to adjust their investment strategies accordingly, whether it be accumulating assets during bear markets or taking profits during bull markets.

By grasping the concepts of market cycles and timing, business owners can develop a Crypto Millionaire Mindset. With the right knowledge and mindset, business owners can seize the immense investment opportunities offered by cryptocurrencies and potentially achieve financial prosperity.

Understanding the Bull and Bear Markets:

In the ever-evolving world of cryptocurrency investment opportunities, it is crucial for business owners to understand the concept of bull and bear markets.

These terms are commonly used to describe the overall market sentiment and can significantly influence investment decisions.

A bull market refers to a period of time when the prices of cryptocurrencies are generally rising. During this phase, investor confidence is high, and there is an overall positive sentiment in the market. One can benefit greatly from a bull market by taking advantage of the upward price movements and making profitable investments. Also note the bull markets are followed by periods of price corrections. Some indicators of a bull market include increasing trading volumes, positive news surrounding cryptocurrencies, and a general uptrend in prices

A bear market represents a period of time when the prices of cryptocurrencies are generally falling. This phase is marked by pessimism and fear among investors, leading to a decrease in demand and, subsequently, a decline in prices. While a bear market may seem discouraging, it can present lucrative opportunities with a long-term investment mindset. By strategically buying cryptocurrencies at lower prices, one can position for significant profits when the market eventually recovers.signs of a bear market may include decreasing trading volumes, negative news impacting the cryptocurrency industry, and a general downtrend in prices.

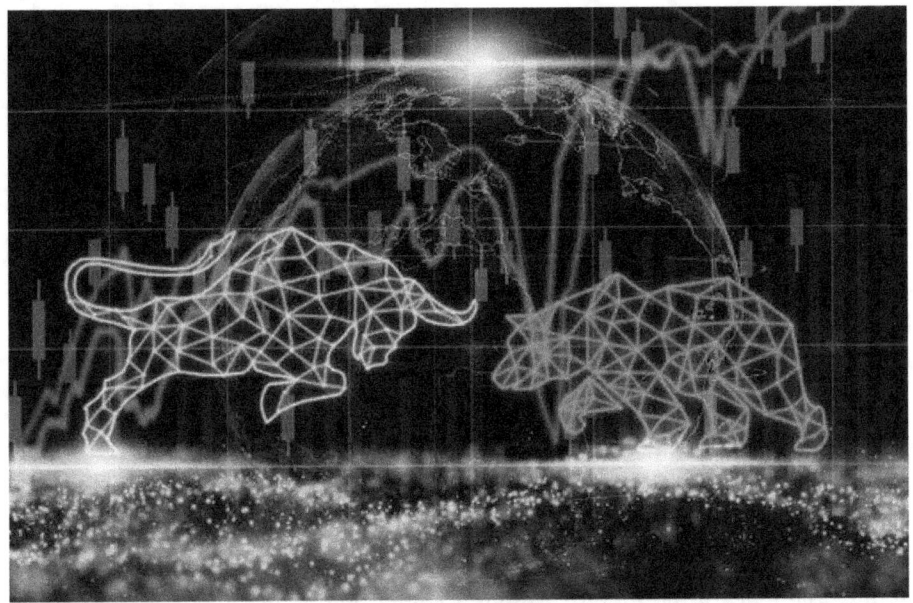

In conclusion, recognizing bull and bear markets is essential for business owners looking to invest in cryptocurrency. Understanding these market trends allows for informed decision-making and the ability to capitalize on profitable opportunities. By staying alert to market indicators and employing effective analysis techniques, business owners can develop a crypto millionaire mindset and unlock the full potential of their investments in the dynamic world of cryptocurrencies.

Identifying Market Manipulation and Scams

In the fast-paced world of cryptocurrency investment opportunities, it is crucial for business owners to navigate the market with caution and vigilance. While the potential for significant returns is undeniable, so too are the risks associated with market manipulation and scams. In this chapter, we will explore the various tactics employed by fraudsters and provide you with essential knowledge to identify and avoid falling victim to these schemes.

Market manipulation, a deceptive practice intended to artificially influence the price of a cryptocurrency, is a common occurrence in the crypto space. One way scammers achieve this is through "pump and dump" schemes, where they artificially inflate the price of a specific coin through coordinated buying, creating a false sense of demand. Once the price reaches a certain peak, the scammers sell their holdings, causing the price to plummet and leaving unsuspecting investors with significant losses.One of the ways to reduce your investments risks is to be updated regularly and invest in the TOP stable currencies namely as explained in Chapter 1.

WHAT IS BITCOIN ETF's :

What is the big deal about a spot ETF?
As all of you know, there are plenty of ways to get spot exposure to bitcoin already. Typically that means buying it directly from an exchange like Coinbase, Kraken, or Robinhood. But these come with some fine print. For one, the fees can be relatively expensive. On the one hand, some spot ETFs will waive fees for the first 6-12 months (more on that in the next section), while exchanges like Coinbase cost an eye-watering 300bps for small retail purchases. Plus as you all know it takes some effort to sign up for an account at one of these exchanges and link a bank account. Spot ETFs will eliminate the need for any of that as you will be able to direct a brokerage account to make an allocation with the click of a button. Second, as we all saw from the collapse of FTX, Voyager, Celsius, BlockFi, and others counterparty risk is a real thing. That will not be an issue in the regulated field of spot bitcoin ETFs, especially when it involves blue chip players like BlackRock and Fidelity. Some of the prominent ETFs are mentioned below with their fees, waiver details and Exchanges.

Name	Ticker	Fee (after Waiver)	Waiver Details	Exchange	Most Recent Filing	Custodian
Bitwise Bitcoin ETP Trust (Re-filing)	BITB	0.0% (0.20%)	6 Months &/or $1 Billion	NYSE	1/9/24	Coinbase
ARK 21Shares Bitcoin ETF (Re-filing)	ARKB	0.0% (0.25%)	6 Months &/or $1 Billion	CBOE	1/9/24	Coinbase
Invesco Galaxy Bitcoin ETF (Re-filing)	BTCO	0.0% (0.39%)	6 Months &/or $5 Billion	CBOE	1/9/24	Coinbase
Wisdomtree Bitcoin Trust (Re-filing)	BTCW	0.0% (0.30%)	6 Months &/or $1 Billion	CBOE	1/9/24	Coinbase
Valkyrie Bitcoin Fund (Re-filing)	BRRR	0.0% (0.49%)	3 Months	Nasdaq	1/9/24	Coinbase
iShares Bitcoin Trust	IBIT	0.20% (0.30%)	12 Months &/or $5 Billion	Nasdaq	1/9/24	Coinbase
VanEck Bitcoin Trust (Re-filing)	HODL	0.25%	None	CBOE	1/9/24	Gemini
Franklin Bitcoin ETF	EZBC	0.29%	None	CBOE	1/9/24	Coinbase
Fidelity Wise Origin Bitcoin Trust (Re-filing)	FBTC	0.39%	None	CBOE	1/9/24	Fidelity
Hashdex Bitcoin ETF Strategy Change	DEFI	0.90%	None	NYSE	12/26/23	BitGo
Grayscale Bitcoin Trust (Re-file) Conversion	GBTC	1.5%	None	NYSE	1/9/24	Coinbase

Source: Bloomberg Intelligence, SEC.gov

Bloomberg

What is going to happen to the price of bitcoin?

Bitcoin has a nasty habit of buying rumors and selling news. It happened twice in 2021 when Coinbase went public in April and then futures ETFs began trading in October.

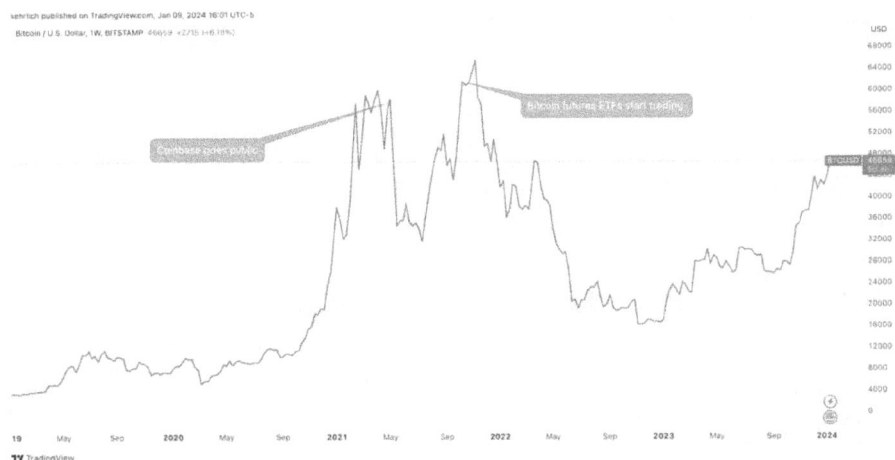

Source: Forbes dated 09th Jan 2024.

Will that happen again? It probably depends on how much new money comes in right away. I've seen predictions all over the map, and to be honest nobody knows. I do know that the conditions are right for a tight move up should there be a jump. The total amount of bitcon on exchanges is the lowest that it has been in four years, according to data from Glassnode. I would not be surprised if billions do not flow in right away. Some investors and brokerage houses may want to see how these products trade first. Remember, just because the

SEC says that these products are now legal does not mean that brokers must support them on day one.

With that being the case. If new money does not fly in at the start, bitcoin could drag a little. Based on technical charts, which already show bitcoin to be slightly overbought, the next support levels will be around $41,000 and then $33,000. Therefore, given that bitcoin has surged more than 50% over the past few months, you may want to consider taking some profits off of the table with the expectation of buying back in after the dust settles from these expected launches. However, the long term story sounds of great potential with the third Bitcon halving coming around mid April 2024, long term investors could consider the pull backs as great opportunity to invest in the prominent 7 cryptocurrencies in a staggered or scalping manner. The scalping technique or phased investment helps once to average out on DCA(Dollar cost averaging).

Current Market situation:

The approval of a spot bitcoin ETF by the US Securities and Exchange Commission (SEC) is a landmark achievement for the cryptocurrency industry, especially for investors and crypto enthusiasts. This decision is significant as it potentially bridges the gap between traditional finance and the evolving world of cryptocurrency, making bitcoin more accessible to general investors. A bitcoin ETF, long considered a milestone for bitcoin, is expected to enhance its legitimacy and could increase its demand and value.

This para into the nuances of spot bitcoin ETFs, aiming to provide a comprehensive understanding of what this development means for investors. From its implications on the cryptocurrency market to how it fits into a diversified investment portfolio, we aim to cover everything an investor needs to know about this new and exciting investment opportunity.

What is a spot bitcoin ETF?

A spot bitcoin ETF is an exchange-traded fund that tracks the current market price of bitcoin, also known as its spot price. Unlike ETFs that are based on bitcoin futures contracts, a spot bitcoin ETF invests directly in bitcoin.

This approach provides a more regulated and straightforward way for mainstream investors to include bitcoin in their portfolios. While management fees and brokerage commissions are applicable, these costs can be more economical than the expenses and complexities involved in directly purchasing and holding bitcoin. This type of ETF simplifies the process of investing in bitcoin, making it more accessible to a broader range of investors.

The past: Initial SEC stance on spot bitcoin ETFs

For several years, the US Securities and Exchange Commission (SEC) initially resisted the approval of spot bitcoin ETFs. Their primary concern revolved around the regulation of bitcoin markets. The SEC argued that the bitcoin market was too unregulated and susceptible to manipulation, posing a risk of fraud to average investors. They believed that the lack of sufficient monitoring and surveillance capabilities in the bitcoin spot market compared to the more regulated bitcoin futures market made spot bitcoin ETFs a less secure option for investors

The present: Shift in SEC's position

The SEC's change of heart regarding spot bitcoin ETFs came after a federal court ruling, which criticized their earlier rejections as inconsistent. The court pointed out the contradiction in approving bitcoin futures ETFs while denying spot bitcoin ETFs despite the close price correlation between the futures and spot markets. This ruling and evolving market circumstances led SEC Chairman Gary Gensler to acknowledge a change in conditions. Consequently, Gensler stated that the commission's previous rationale no longer applied, leading to the approval of spot bitcoin ETFs. However, Gensler clarified that this decision was specific to bitcoin and did not imply a broader acceptance of other crypto-related products or a general change in the SEC's stance on cryptocurrencies.

The Road ahead:

The reaction to Bitcoin's correction following the spot ETF approval has been fear and panic.Which only makes sense if you ignore everything but recent price action.But if you've been reading up on your Weiss Crypto Daily updates, you'll know there's so much more at work in the crypto market. It was sparked by the wave of investors selling the news following the spot Bitcoin ETF approval.What fear mongers fail to mention is the fact that the four months leading up to that approval marked one of the longest 80-day rally in Bitcoin history. (source coinGecko)

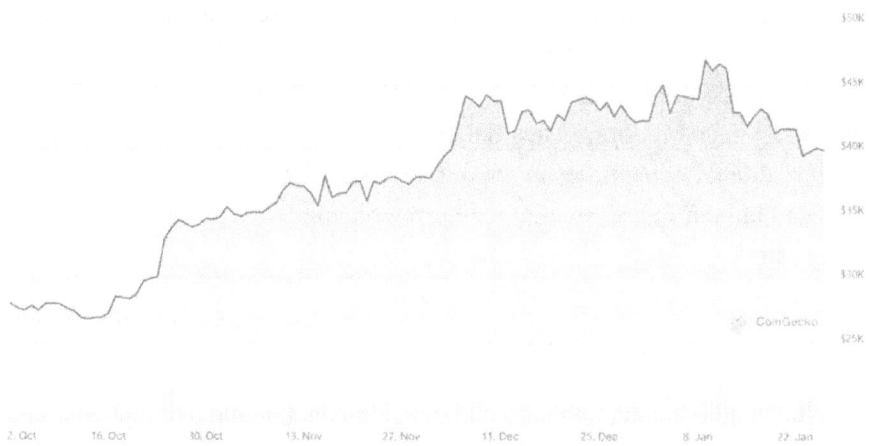

That means Bitcoin was already in rally mode and ready to transition to the pullback phase of its 80-day cycle going into the approval announcement. Indeed, it's likely that anticipation and hype kept Bitcoin at those elevated levels longer than it otherwise would have been.You'd think after such a stellar performance in the last quarter of 2023, people would be chilling with some bubbly, celebrating the dawn of a new crypto bull market in early 2024.

Naturally, there was the wave of initial "sell the news" traders looking to grab gains at the top. But there is still selling pressure from Grayscale clients. Many are seeking to get away from Grayscale's high fees, especially as there are 10 other ETFs with far more manageable fees.

The cycle of inflated expectations followed by the inevitable disappointment.The whole "buy the rumor, sell the news" spiel couldn't be more spot-on.

And that's why I'm not losing sleep over it.

As a seasoned cycles analyst, I knew the party had to end sometime. Seeing Bitcoin's meteoric rise from $25,000 to almost $50,000, I was ready for the tide of disappointment and the ensuing sell-off.

But I have another reason for my optimism beyond being able to anticipate the correction: ***There's a perfect supply/demand storm brewing on the horizon that could send Bitcoin soaring.***

The increased demand from the ETFs isn't going away any time soon. But the Bitcoin halving expected to come in late April promises an even smaller circulating supply.When those two conditions are met, Bitcoin will have all the fuel it needs to go even higher.

So, while the market takes a breather and the latecomers fret, those in the know like you should see this as the golden opportunity.

Once your portfolio is ready, all you have to do is wait to ride the next wave of the crypto bull market.

SUMMARY: In this CHAPTER we have tried to identify the major current trends in the market, although there are over 1200 crypto currencies, I have highlighted some of the major ones . Those of you who would like to take higher risks for a higher risk reward ratio, there are other altcoins which are present in the crypto space and some of them are like Hidden gems with Space rocket potential which can go either way , we will cover some of the new upcoming ones in our next book, As for the high risk takers. Higher returns also include high risks, for the Beginners, it could be prudent to stick to the basic or fundamentals of Investing, be with the Market leaders.....

HOW TO GET STARTED ,WHERE DO WE START ???
TRUST THE ABOVE CHAPTERS HAVE GIVEN SOME GOOD INSIGHTS?
....????
LETS SUMMARISE THE STEPS TO BE TAKEN IN OUR FINAL CHAPTER

CHAPTER 6 : .....FINAL STEPS TOWARDS YOUR MILLIONAIRE MINDSET

GETTING STARTED IN THE CRYPTO WORLD: THE PROCESS .....
As a Investor, we should know what are the steps after our research so that timely steps can be taken, we do not recommend the FOMO effect (FEAR OF MISSING OUT). However, being updated and in sync with market trends can make your process towards crypto millionaire with some of the best coins a reality sooner than expected.

Lets look at the below illustration to understand the process, so as we can understand, the need to open an account with the crypto exchange, second step would be which are the currencies you have decided to invest, thirdly as per your risk appetite, how much you can invest and store in a wallet.

Warning or Words of wisdom, keep yourself updated on a regular basis to know the trends and opportunities in the crypto space.

 CRYPTOREACH

How to Invest in Crypto
Currency

SELECT A CRYPTOCURRENCY EXCHANGE

CHOOSE WHAT CRYPTOCURRENC Y TO INVEST IN

CONSIDER STORAGE AND DIGITAL WALLET OPTION

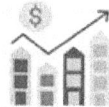

DECIDE HOW MUCH TO INVEST

STAY UP TO DATE WITH INDUSTRY

MANAGE YOUR INVESTMENT

Source: Crypto reach.

The above would not be complete without giving some perspective on the prominent crypto exchanges to open a account, lets look at the Topmost few exchanges in the image below,

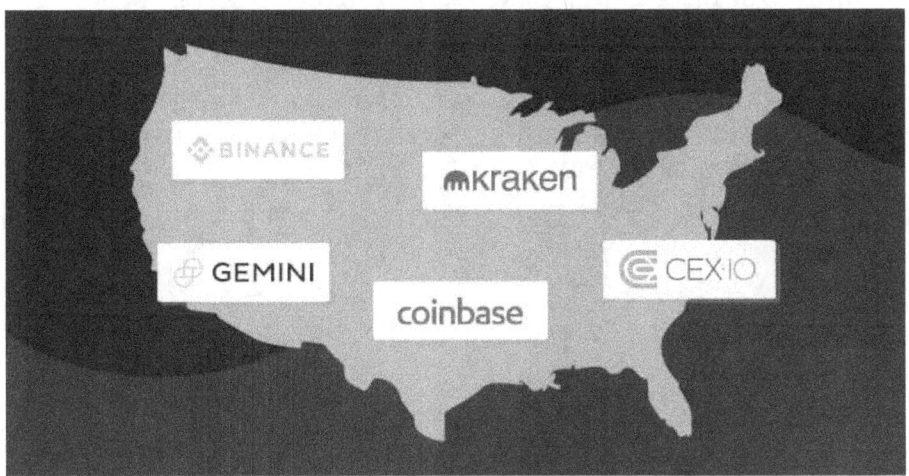

RATINGS FOR SOME OF THE BEST CRYPTO CURRENCIES TO INVEST:

SUMMARY:

In this CHAPTER, we have seen what are the steps to follow to have a crypto account, the major exchanges and the ratings for some of the best rated crypto currencies.

we have tried to identify some of the best among over 1200 crypto currencies, I have highlighted some of the major ones especially for the low or medium risk takers. Those of you who would like to take higher risks for a higher risk reward ratio, there are other altcoins which are present in the crypto space, we will cover some of the Next Gen Altcoins in our next book as the volatility of some of the coins is from Zero to Hero or vice versa.. Higher returns as one knows include high risks and so the more stable coins have been highlighted with almost 80% market share of the crypto space.....

As a wise investor looking for stable growth once can study these for good potential gains with short, medium or long term gains!!

Till then Happy Investing!!!!

DISCLAIMER:

ALL INVESTMENTS INCLUDING THE CRYPTO CURRENCIES ARE SUBJECT TO MARKET RISKS WITH POTENTIAL ON EITHER SIDES. THE AUTHOR DOES NOT PROMOTE ANY SPECIFIC CRYPTO ASSET FOR INVESTMENTS, AND HAS SUGGESTED SOME OF THE LEADING CRYPTO CURRENCIES FOR THEIR POTENTIAL AND PAST HISTORIC DATA FOR EDUCATIONAL AND OR INVESTMENT PURPOSES AS PER THEIR OWN INDIVIDUAL DECISION. EACH INDIVIDUAL COULD TAKE SOME PROFESSIONAL ADVISE BEFORE INVESTING. EACH ONE IS SOLELY RESPONSIBLE FOR ANY INVESTMENT DECISIONS MADE IN THE CRYTO SPACE.

www.ingramcontent.com/pod-product-compliance
Lightning Source LLC
Chambersburg PA
CBHW071003290526
45795CB00005B/1759